Gilbert Galaxy, Space Hero

by Christopher Stitt

illustrated by Ken Rinkel

Harcourt Achieve

Rigby • Saxon • Steck-Vaughn

www.HarcourtAchieve.com
1.800.531.5015

Characters

Gilbert

Clunk

Princess Nova

Tyro

Contents

Chapter 1

Distress Call

"There's a call coming in," beeped Clunk.

Gilbert was excited. This was his first call. A fuzzy picture of a girl popped onto the screen. "I need help!" she cried.

"What's the problem?" asked Gilbert.

"My name is Princess Nova," said the girl.
"I'm being held prisoner in my castle on the
planet Floop."

Gilbert asked, "Who's holding you?"

"My captors are . . . Help, they're here."
The screen went blank.

"Come in, Princess," shouted Gilbert.

Clunk put his metal hand on Gilbert's shoulder. "The link's been lost, sir."

"This is my first job as Gilbert Galaxy, Space Hero," said Gilbert.

Gilbert shook a small, red, furry thing. "Wake up, Tyro. We have a job."

Tyro yawned. "A job? What job?"

"We're off to save a princess."

Chapter 2

To The Rescue

Gilbert and Tyro rushed to the Galaxy Gismo. The super-fast spaceship had just been finished.

"We haven't tested the ship yet," bleeped Clunk.

"I've never known a robot who worries so much," said Gilbert.

Gilbert's mom called from the kitchen,
"Where are you going, Gilbert?"

"For a quick spin, Mom."

"Don't go far. Supper's nearly ready."

"Don't worry, Mom." Gilbert strapped on his seatbelt.

Tyro flipped some buttons. "The course for Floop is set."

Clunk's eye flashed. "Floop is so far away. We might not be back for supper."

"You're wasting time, Clunk," urged Gilbert.

Clunk started the engines. In a cloud of smoke, the Galaxy Gismo took off into space.

A large green planet loomed up ahead.

"Is that Floop?" asked Gilbert.

"Yes," buzzed Clunk. "This is Floop."

"See that forest," said Gilbert. "We should land there."

"We should land closer to the castle," said Tyro.

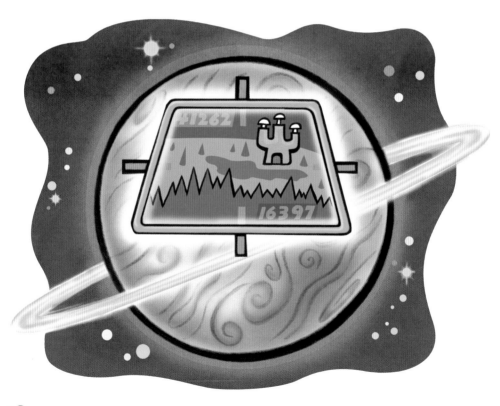

"No, we need to sneak up on them," said Gilbert.

The Galaxy Gismo rumbled as it landed.

"Don't worry, Princess. Gilbert Galaxy is here to save you."

Chapter 3

Knee Deep in Trouble

Gilbert opened the hatch. "Follow me."

Clunk stayed close to Gilbert as they headed into the dark forest. "I have a bad feeling about this," Clunk said, shaking.

"Stop rattling, Clunk," whispered Gilbert. "You'll give us away."

"I can see daylight ahead," Tyro pointed.

The three heroes ran into the clearing. They came to a halt at the edge of a huge swamp. It stood between them and the castle.

A slimy, green hand reached out of the swamp and grabbed Tyro's foot. "Help! Something's got me."

Gilbert drew his laser.

"Drop it!" a voice called from behind.

Gilbert turned. They were surrounded by frogs with weapons. Gilbert dropped his laser. Tyro vanished into the swamp with a plop.

Chapter 4

Amphibious

A frog grabbed Gilbert.

"Where's Tyro?" demanded Gilbert. "He can't swim."

"Hold your breath," hissed the frog. He dragged Gilbert into the swampy water. Gilbert hoped they didn't bring Clunk. He might rust.

"I'm here on a mission," said Gilbert as they dropped down inside a giant bubble.

"Quiet," croaked the frog. "Save it for the King."

Their bubble floated up onto grassy ground and burst.

Tyro was already there. Another bubble
burst, and there stood a scared Clunk.

A huge frog stood on a platform. "I'm King
Amphib. Why do you disturb the Frogblops
of Floop?"

"My name is Gilbert Galaxy, Space Hero. We're here to save Princess Nova."

"The Princess is in danger?" gasped the King.

"She is," beeped Clunk. He played them her message.

"We need to get into the castle,"
Gilbert pleaded.

"That tunnel will take you into the castle,"
said King Amphib pointing.

"I hope there are no spiders,"
rattled Clunk.

"Which room is the Princess in?"
asked Tyro.

"In the tower," Gilbert decided. "That's
where prisoners are always kept."

Chapter 5

Tower of Terror

"Look!" Gilbert pointed. "A staircase."

Tyro and Clunk followed Gilbert up the steep stairs. They stopped at a door.

Gilbert knocked. "Are you there, Princess?"

The door opened. Princess Nova stared at Gilbert. "You came!"

"No job is too hard for Gilbert Galaxy. Let's get you out of here!"

"She's not going anywhere," boomed a woman's voice.

"But, Mom," moaned Princess Nova, "Gilbert came to save me."

"Your mom is keeping you prisoner?" gasped Tyro.

"Princess Nova wouldn't eat her peas, so I sent her to her room," said the Queen.

"We came all this way because you wouldn't eat your veggies!" Gilbert couldn't believe it.

King Amphib came running up the stairs. "Is the Princess safe?"

"She wouldn't eat her peas," said Gilbert.

"She's a bit of a brat," whispered King Amphib.

King Nova gave Gilbert some money.
"To cover your expenses."

Gilbert sat in the Galaxy Gismo and counted
the gold coins. "Twenty! Not a bad trip
after all."

Clunk looked at his watch. "It's nearly suppertime."

"Put us into extra hyper-drive, Clunk," said Gilbert.

"We'll all eat our peas tonight, too," added Tyro, laughing.

And so goes the life of a space hero.

Glossary

amphibious
able to live on land and water

brat
a badly behaved child

captors
people who hold others prisoner

expenses
money spent while doing a job

hatch
the small door in a spaceship

laser
a powerful beam of light

link
a connection which allows people to communicate

loomed
appeared as a large shape

mission
a very important job

spin
a fast drive or ride

Christopher Stitt

Q: What do space heroes shave with?
A: Laser blades.

Q: Why are all aliens such good gardeners?
A: They have lots of green thumbs.

Q: What is an alien's favorite snack?
A: Astronuts.

How fantastic would it be to have your very own spaceship? I always dreamed of being able to zoom around space like a super hero.

Ken Rinkel